Jesus and Jonah

J.W. McGarvey

President of the College of the Bible
Lexington, Kentucky

Jesus and Jonah

P.O. Box 6259, Chillicothe, Ohio 45601

www.dewardpublishing.com

Sections 1–3 of *Jesus and Jonah* were first published in J. W. McGarvey's Biblical Criticism column in *The Christian Standard* in 1895: "Jesus and Jonah" (August 31, p. 835; September 7, p. 859; September 14, p. 885; September 21, p. 909); "Is the Story of Jonah Incredible" (September 28, p. 933; October 5, p. 957; 12 October, p. 981); "Driver on the Book of Jonah" (October 26, p. 1029); "The Date of the Book of Jonah" (November 2, p. 1053). These essays, with the previously unpublished Section 4, were issued in book form by Standard Publishing in 1896.

In this edition, minor changes have been made to the original text. All of these changes are stylistic preferences of the publisher and do not affect the content herein. The vast majority of these changes have been in the style of verse citations (*e.g.*, I Pet. iv: 11 to 1 Pet 4.11) and punctuation (*e.g.*, -- to —).

ISBN: 978-0-9819703-2-5

To the Eminent Hebraist,
Professor William Henry Green,
of Princeton,
The Acknowledged Leader of
American Scholars throughout a Whole Generation
in Defending The Bible Against Destructive Criticism.

This Defense of One of its Smallest Books,
is with His Approval Gratefully Inscribed.

Contents

Foreword

It is good to see the re-issue of McGarvey's book on *Jesus and Jonah.* It is a serious and sober look at an issue that has not gone away since his time. If anything, the issue of the historicity of the Biblical narratives is even more of an issue today, since we now have the Jesus Seminar, the Copenhagen school, and other such groups who advocate an absolute minimalist approach to the Bible, and who publicly proclaim (as the result of their approach) that the Biblical stories basically never happened. The names of the advocates have changed since McGarvey's day, but the basic, thorough-going historical skepticism of the humanistic approach to the Bible has not.

This book is valuable first because of its main point. The author showed, in arguments that were both simple and razor-sharp, that the denial of the historicity of Jonah's story makes Jesus either a liar or a fool. While it would not surprise us to hear atheists of all ages making such charges, McGarvey's point is that it is self-contradictory for theologians and Bible students to accept or advocate a position that implicitly reaches the same conclusion. His book is devoted to the proposition that if we are going to approach the Bible at all, we must do so on the Bible's terms. Or, if you will, if you want the Jesus of the New Testament, then everything that he said comes with him. You may reject the entire package, or you may accept it all, but no middle ground is possible.

The book is also valuable for its method. The author's procedure in the case of Jesus' statement about Jonah applies to everything Jesus said about the Old Testament. This has far-reaching consequences for the inspiration, canonicity, and proper interpretation of the Old Testament, but also has tremendous implications for our reading of the New Testament. To accept what Jesus said about Jonah is ultimately to accept the entire Bible as the word of God.

McGarvey's remarks also bring us back to a time when believers were able to refute destructive critics of the Bible in clear, strong arguments. In a world where students are increasingly encouraged and expected to hold to their own views quietly, and even uncritically, this book is like a breath of fresh air. It is straightforward in its confrontation with the issues, and (unlike the critics) the author never loses sight of the main point.

J. W. McGarvey believed that his book had not been refuted in his day (see his *Short Essays in Biblical Criticism* (Cincinnati: Standard Publishing Co., 1910) 153-55). We are of the same opinion almost a hundred years later.

David McClister | Florida College
September 2009

Preface

The contents of this volume, with the exception of the dissertation on "The Three Days and Three Nights," were first published in the Critical Department of *The Christian Standard.* They are republished in more permanent form at the request of many readers, and with the hope that they will thus have a more extended circulation. If they shall cause any to more highly appreciate the inimitable story of Jonah, and to have a firmer faith in the utterances of Jesus, they will serve the purpose for which both publications have been made.

The Author
March, 1896

Introduction

by Professor William Henry Green
Princeton Theological Seminary

The attitude of the Lord Jesus Christ toward the Old Testament is a source of great embarrassment to those who acknowledge him as a Divine Teacher, and yet are not in accord with his views on this subject. The puzzle is to reconcile the uniqueness of his person as the incarnate Son of God, the uniqueness of his claim to implicit reverence and confidence, and his supreme authority as a Divine Teacher, with the admission that he was or could be mistaken in any of his teachings, or that he ever gave his sanction to the errors or mistakes of others. The difficulty created by his attestation given to other parts of the Old Testament recurs in equal measure in the language which he uses respecting the Book of Jonah. The attempt to save his authority by minimizing the force of his words can neither be acceptable to him, nor can it answer its mistaken purpose.

There is no reason for discrediting the Book of Jonah, unless it is to be found in the contents of the book itself. The extraordinary and supernatural occurrences here related can not be pronounced incredible by him who believes in the reality of the miracles recorded elsewhere in the Bible, unless their nature is such, or the occasion is such as to justify any one in affirming that they are mere freaks of power with no worthy end, mere prodigies, so out of analogy with all true miracles, that it is altogether insupposable that God could, or would, have wrought them. But how can any one venture upon such an assertion in view of the fact that the Lord Jesus speaks of them without in any way suggesting that they were incompatible with the character of God, and that he even puts the most marvelous of them in relation to his own stupendous miracle of rising from the dead, the one a sign to the Ninevites, the other to the men of his own generation.

1. A Symposium Reviewed

I believe it to be universal with critics of the new school and their disciples, to deny the historical reality of the story of Jonah. Those of them who still believe in Jesus Christ, find it necessary to reckon with a statement from his lips, found in Matthew 12.38–41. The passage seems to contain a positive affirmation of the reality of the two events which render the story of Jonah incredible in the judgment of most of these gentlemen, and they have felt the necessity of setting aside in some way its apparent force. The passage reads thus:

> Then certain of the scribes and Pharisees answered him, saying, Master, we would see a sign from thee. But he answered and said unto them, An evil and adulterous generation seeketh after a sign; and there shall no sign be given to it but the sign of Jonah the prophet: for as Jonah was three days and three nights in the belly of the sea monster, so shall the Son of man be three days and three nights in the heart of the earth. The men of Nineveh shall stand up in the judgment with this generation, and shall condemn it: for they repented at the preaching of Jonah; and behold a greater than Jonah is here.

In demanding of Jesus a sign, the scribes and Pharisees denied by implication that any of the multitude of signs which he had wrought were real signs; and their demand was for one of a different kind. In answering that no sign should be given but that of the prophet Jonah, he could not have meant that he would give no more of the kind which he had been giving; for he did give more of these, and in great abundance; but he meant that none should be given of a different kind, except the sign of Jonah. This was different, in that it was wrought *upon* him, and not *by* him, and it was therefore a more direct and manifest exhibition of power from heaven. He explains what he means by the sign of Jonah, by adding: "As Jonah was three days and three nights in the belly of the sea-monster, so shall the Son of man be three days and three nights in the heart of the earth." He then affirms, that because the men of Nineveh repented at the preaching of Jonah, and the men of his own generation repented not at his own greater preaching, the former shall rise up in the judgment and condemn the latter; that is, cause them to receive a severer sentence.

To the great mass of readers in every age and country, it has appeared that Jesus here assumes as a settled fact that Jonah was in the great fish as described in the Book of Jonah, and that the Ninevites actually repented under the influence of his preaching. So obvious does this appear that probably no human being has ever raised a question about it until after he has reached the conclusion that these two events are incredible. Then he must get rid of this obvious meaning, or deny the truthfulness of an assertion made by Jesus Christ. Many attempts at the former have been made in recent years, and I propose, in this volume, to put every one of them to the test, so far as they have come under my notice. I do this, not because it is a matter of supreme importance in itself to know whether Jonah was swallowed by the fish and thrown up again, but because the question involves principles of interpretation which affect every statement by our Lord with reference to events mentioned in the Old Testament, and in reference to the authorship of some of its books. It is really a question as to whether Jesus is to be received as a competent witness respecting historical and literary matters of the ages which preceded his own. If he is not, then the conception of his person and his powers which believers have hitherto entertained must undergo very serious modifications, even if it shall not be totally abandoned. One of the editors of the *Biblical World,* Professor Shailer Mathews, has felt the need of some efforts to settle this question, and in the number of that magazine for June, 1895, he published a symposium, the origin of which he states in these words:

> In order to learn how far this passage, with its explicit reference, is held by the teachers of religion to set Christ's seal upon the story of Jonah, letters were sent to a considerable number of representative pastors and teachers, asking them to give the readers of the *Biblical World* their opinions. The following replies have been received in time for publication in this number. (p. 417)

Eight replies are published, contributed respectively by Lemuel C. Barnes, Pittsburg, Pa; J. Henry Thayer, Harvard Divinity School; Franklin Johnson, University of Chicago; William DeW. Hyde, Bowdoin College; Philip S. Moxom, Springfield, Mass.; Rush Rhees, Newtown Theological Institution; Amory H. Bradford, First Congregational Church, Montclair, N.J.; and C.J.H. Ropes, Bangor Theological Seminary.

The editor sums up the result of the symposium in the following statement at the close of the series:

> It is not difficult to formulate the common belief found in these statements of men who differ greatly in their attitude toward many theological questions. It is this: Christ's use of the experience of Jonah as an illustration in no way gives his sanction to the view that the Book of Jonah is history. (p. 430)

It strikes me as rather singular that the editor here speaks of "Christ's use of the experience of Jonah," when Jonah had no such experience. Does the editor here unconsciously betray the fact that the reality of this experience is so impressed on his own mind that he unintentionally concedes it while arguing against it?

I confess myself ignorant of the special qualifications of all these eight scholars, with the exception of Professor Thayer, of Hartford, whose reputation is international; but I assume from the positions which they occupy, and from the choice made of them by the editor, that they are all men of competent attainments. I shall, therefore, treat their positions, and the reasons by which they defend them, as the best that can be said by men on their side of the question.

Professor Thayer is the only one of the eight who says plainly what he thinks of the Book of Jonah. He says:

> In my judgment, the characteristics of the Book of Jonah favor the opinion that it is an apologue, or "religious novel," a composition didactic in its aim. How large a historic element it contains can hardly be determined. (417)

It seems from this that the book, though a novel, contains a historic element; but how large this element is, the Professor can not determine. As foot is sometimes stranger than fiction, why not suppose that Jonah's experience in the fish is the historical element, and that the novel was woven around this central fact? Nothing in the sentence just quoted, or in all that the Professor has said, conflicts with this supposition; and yet this is apparently the very thing of all in the book which he would most seriously doubt.

While Professor Thayer can not determine the amount of historic matter in the book, Professor Hyde is equally unable to determine what Jesus meant by his allusion to it. He says:

> I should rather not commit myself to an exegesis of such a highly figurative passage as Matthew 12.39–40. A man's exegesis of such a passage as that is bound to be simply a reading into it of his general conception of things. What it says is as plain as A, BC It requires no exegesis to determine that. It may mean any one of ten thousand things to as many readers. Just precisely what Jesus meant by it we shall never know. (419)

This Professor has certainly made a new discovery. It is the discovery of a fact which no man ever before suspected, the fact that this passage, the meaning of which has hitherto given commentators no serious difficulty, is so obscure that it may mean any one of ten thousand things to as many readers; and that what Jesus really meant, "we shall never know." If we have to choose between ten thousand different meanings, I am afraid that we shall never know, sure enough. But perhaps the figures can be reduced a little, as in case of the man who was starting the song,—

> "My soul be on thy guard,
> Ten thousand foes arise."

When he got to "ten thousand," the tune suddenly rose so high that he could not reach it; but after he had made two or three vain attempts, a neighbor whispered: *"Put it down to five hundred and you can reach it."* Perhaps, when our Professor gets over the excitement of his new discovery, he will put his figures down. Scientific critics should aim at exactness.

One of these writers, Mr. Moxom, cuts the Gordian knot, by pronouncing the remark about Jonah and the fish a spurious addition to Matthew's narrative. He says:

> I agree with Wendt that verse 40 is an interpolation. The sign to which Jesus refers in verse 39 is evidently the prophet preaching repentance. As Jonah preached to the Ninevites, so Jesus preached to the men of his time. There are coherency and force in the passage, verses 39 and 41 if we leave out verse 40. Verse 40 introduces a new idea, and one that is not strictly congruous with the others. (420)

I suppose that a meaning of the passage is implied in these remarks, which we might count as one of Professor Hyde's ten thousand. But we shall not dwell upon it; for the writer virtually takes back what I have quoted when he says in the very next sentence: "There is, as far as I know, no evidence that verse 40 is a gloss." I suppose he means, no evidence other than conjecture; and in this he is right. Having conceded this, he goes outside the laws of textual criticism in holding the passage to be spurious. A theory which demands the erasure of Scripture to make room for itself is self-evidently unscriptural.

Only one of these writers, Professor Ropes, ventures to say explicitly what Jesus thought of the Book of Jonah. He says:

> I have no doubt Jesus supposed the Book of Jonah was historical, and have no objection to believing that he thought the same of the sea-monster miracle, though the evidence is less cogent. But the attempt to use such facts in the higher criticism controversy seems to be founded on a radically erroneous view of Christ's knowledge while on earth. (429)

According to this writer, then, Jesus labored under a mistake in regard to the book; for he supposed it to be historical, when it was not. Yet the same writer says in the next paragraph:

> Throughout his ministry, Jesus showed full knowledge of all that belonged to the revelation he brought, and exercised the prophetic gifts of insight into character and future events.

This concession falsifies the preceding statement; for, if Jesus showed full knowledge of all that belonged to the revelation which he brought, then he had full knowledge of all the Old Testament records, so far, at least, as he made use of them. But he did make a most important use of the two principal incidents recorded in the Book of Jonah. He did suppose, says our professor, that this book was historical; and his full knowledge implies that what he thus supposed he also knew. He knew, then, that the Book of Jonah was historical; and the attempt to use such facts as arguments in the higher criticism controversy is not, as he affirms, founded on "an erroneous view of Christ's knowledge while on earth."

This writer has another remark, in the line of the first one quoted above, which I must notice.

> But, receiving his authority absolutely in the spheres of religion and morality, I do not see why his knowledge of the literary history of the Old Testament should have differed essentially from that of his contemporaries, any more than his knowledge of chemistry or astronomy. (430)

I could better estimate this remark if I understood the writer to hold that the Old Testament has no more connection with "the spheres of religion and morality" than chemistry and astronomy have; but if he receives, as he says he does, the divine authority, of Christ in the spheres of morality and religion, then he must receive as true those records in the Old Testament on the truth of which Jesus based certain of his moral and religious teachings.

This inconsistency in Professor Ropes is but an illustration of the fact which will again and again appear as we proceed with this symposium, that no man can accept the divine authority of Jesus, and reject his endorsement of the Old Testament, without self-contradiction. I wonder, by the by, how this Professor ascertained that Jesus was as ignorant as his contemporaries were of chemistry and astronomy?

Before I notice the direct arguments by which these eight writers attempt to make good their common position, I wish first to settle, if possible, what our Saviour meant by "the sign of Jonah," in the assertion, "No sign shall be given but the sign of Jonah the prophet." Some of them take the position that Jonah's preaching to the Ninevites was the sign. Thus Mr. Moxom says:

> The sign to which Jesus refers, in verse 39 is evidently the prophet preaching repentance. As Jonah preached to the Ninevites, so Jesus preached to the men of his time. ...In brief, then, I take the meaning to be this: Jesus declines to furnish any sign in response to the demand of the Scribes and Pharisees, save the obvious one of himself preaching repentance to them, as Jonah preached to the Ninevites. (420)

To the same effect Professor Ropes says:

> The question is: How did Jonah become a sign? Matthew replies, by the sea-monster miracle, analogous to Christ's resurrection. But Luke 11.30 may mean that Jonah was a sign like Christ, by preaching repentance in view of coming judgement. Conservatives underestimate the strength of this view by assuming it implies that Jonah's sign was only a call to repentance. Jonah cried, "Yet forty days and Nineveh shall be overthrown." So Christ proclaimed: "Repent, or Jerusalem shall be overthrown"; and in conduct and destiny the Jews strongly contrast with the Ninevites. (428)

If the view of Luke's meaning here expressed is correct, it contradicts the meaning ascribed to Matthew; and I am not sure which view the writer really takes. He certainly understands Matthew correctly; or rather, he understands correctly the words of Jesus reported by Matthew; for when Jesus says, "No sign shall be given save the sign of Jonah," then immediately adds: "For as Jonah was in the belly of the sea monster three days and three nights, so shall the Son of man be three days and three nights in the heart of the earth," he certainly explains by the last remark what he means by the sign of Jonah. His own resurrection, after entombment for three days, is called the sign of Jonah, because of the similarity of the two miracles. This view is confirmed by the consideration that it was undoubtedly a miraculous sign which the scribes and Pharisees demanded; and the word sign in his answer must be understood in the same sense. It is also confirmed by the consideration that the word rendered sign *(seemeion)* is used almost exclusively in the New Testament for signs of a miraculous character. Indeed, it is the word most usually translated *miracle.* Those works which we call miracles are in the New Testament designated by three different Greek words. They are called mighty works *(dunameis)* because of the divine power exhibited in them. They are called wonders *(terata)* because of the wonder which they excite in the beholder; and they are called signs *(seemeia)*, because they always signify something connected with the will of God.

This view is furthermore confirmed, and made, I think, altogether certain, by the parallel passage in Luke, who quotes another remark of Jesus not reported by Matthew. According to his report, Jesus said: "For even as Jonah was a sign to the Ninevites, so shall also the Son of man be to this generation" (11.30). This is not to be regarded as a different version of the Lord's answer, but only as an additional part of the whole answer, Luke giving one part and Matthew the other, as they very often do. Jesus then asserts that Jonah was a sign to the Ninevites, and he uses the word sign, as we have seen, in the sense of a miracle. But how could Jonah have been a miraculous sign to the Ninevites? He wrought no miracle among them; and his preaching could not have been regarded by them as miraculous until, by means of come separate miraculous sign they were convinced that it was a miraculous prediction. That which made him a sign to the Ninevites must then have been his experience in the fish, connected as it was with the command twice given to go and cry against Nineveh.

One of the eight writers in the symposium, while agreeing with the others on the main question under discussion, avows explicitly the view just stated of the sign of Jonah. He says:

> Apt, therefore, as is the story of Jonah's preaching to illustrate the relation of Jesus to his generation, the wording of Luke 11.30, and what we know of the habits of interpretation in Jesus' day, lead to the conclusion that Luke's more general explanation of the sign of Jonah should be understood in the sense of Matthew's more con-

> crete interpretation; and to the conviction that in the use Jesus made of the words, the sign of Jonah was the deliverance by which he came to be the bearer to Nineveh of the effective warning which led to the people's repentance. The explanation of the sign of Jonah in Matthew 12.40, and Luke 11.30, may be paraphrased thus: As, in the personal experience of Jonah, God proved to him, and afterward to those who heard of his attempted flight, that he was the chosen messenger to the Ninevites; so in the personal experience of the Son of man will God prove to all men that he is the appointed messenger to this generation. This sign in each case is the personal experience of the prophet. (Professor Rhees, 423–424)

Professor Ropes also appears to take the same position, and he quotes with approval a statement of the analogy drawn by Jesus, from the pen of Grass. Here is what he says of this point:

> Perhaps Christ's hearers would naturally think of the sea-monster miracle as the sign of Jonah. And here, too, a good analogy may be found. "In Jonah's life a miracle occurred which could have exerted a controlling influence in vanquishing opposition to him. Yet this didn't help the Ninevites, since they learned nothing about it, but could an event to the decision on the basis of Jonah's preaching alone. Even so in Christ's life, a miracle was about to occur which could exert a controlling influence in drawing men to him. Yet this would no more help this generation to come to a decision than the Jonah sign helped the Ninevites; they must decide on the sole basis of Christ's preaching." (428)

While these two writers differ from two others of the eight in agreeing that the sign of Jonah is the miracle wrought on Jonah's person, the latter, forgetting the very words of Jesus on which he is commenting, declares that the Ninevites were not helped by the sign "since they learned nothing about it." How could it be true, then, that he was a *sign to* the Ninevites? How could an event be a sign to a people when they had never heard of it? And, stranger still, this Professor says that the sign which Jesus was about to give by his resurrection would not help his generation to come to a decision, when the facts in the Book of Acts show that it did help them by causing many thousand to come to a decision under the preaching of the apostles.

But did the Ninevites hear of the sign of Jonah before they repented at his preaching? These men and many others answer, no; and they so answer because the fact is not stated in the Book of Jonah. But while it is not stated in that book, it is stated by Jesus, and there is nothing in the book which conflicts with the statement. On the contrary, the book leaves the way open for the supposition that the news of the miracle reached Nineveh as soon as Jonah did, if not sooner. When he was landed from the mouth of the fish the story immediately became known to the men who found him on the seashore, or to whose house he resorted for food. It is not probable that after fasting and suffering as he did for three days, he was able at once to travel toward home. The story, then, would start ahead of him. When he reached home, we are not told that the Lord renewed immediately the command to go to Nineveh. For aught that is said in the text to the contrary, he may have remained in quiet at home for a week, or a month, before this command came to him; and certainly if God desired the sign to have its effect in advance on the Ninevites, he would delay the command sufficiently for the purpose.

That this view of the sign, and of its conveyance to the Ninevites, is correct, is finally proved by the nature of the analogy which Jesus draws. The sign which he gave to the men of his generation by his resurrection from the dead, was communicated to them in all its details by the apostles. Otherwise it could have been to them no sign. Necessarily, then, if there was a real analogy, and not a sophistical assertion of one, the sign in the person of Jonah must have been communicated to the Ninevites, and it must, as in the other case, have been the controlling evidence on which their faith and their consequent repentance rested. In view of all these considerations, I hope I shall not be considered too confident when I say that the sign of Jonah was the miracle wrought on his person, and that this was certainly known to the Ninevites before they repented at his preaching.

Only one of the eight writers whose symposium I am reviewing, Professor Ropes, denies that Jesus had knowledge of the literary history of the Old Testament above that of his contemporaries.

The other seven, in arguing that his remark about Jonah does not commit him to the historical reality of the story, appeal to what they consider parallel remarks which convey no similar implication. Taking them in the order in which I find them, I shall carefully consider what they say on this point.

Mr. Barnes puts the argument thus:

> Jesus enforced the message upon his lettered hearers with classic point, as in speaking to the students of Princeton Dr. A.J. Gordon might have warned them against the captivating assaults of sin coming in like captors in the wooden horse. The Homeric question would not, thereby, be settled or even raised to consciousness in a healthy mind. (p. 417)

I think that a moment's reflection will show that this last statement would or would not be true according to circumstances. If the students addressed knew that the lecturer disbelieved the story of the wooden horse, they would, of course, understand him as not intending to affirm its truthfulness. But if they believed the story themselves, and knew nothing of his belief, they would unquestionably suppose that he believed as they did. In the latter case, if he did not wish to be understood as indorsing the story, fair dealing with his hearers would demand an intimation at least of his real opinion. In the case of Jesus, his hearers believed the reality of the story of Jonah, and they had not the least thought that Jesus doubted it; when then he said that Jonah was three days and three nights in the belly of the fish, they could not doubt that he believed it; and he made a false impression if he did not.

Next we take Professor Thayer's statement:

> To regard our Lord's use of the narrative as vouching for it as history, is to confound the province and function of a preacher of righteousness with that of a higher critic or of a scientific lecturer. As reasonably might one infer from an allusion in a motherly sermon to William Tell, or Effie Deans, or the Man Without a Country, that the speaker held these personages to be thoroughly historic, and their narrated experiences matters of fact. As warrantably might we make Christ's gratuitous mention (only three verses later) of evil spirits as

> frequenting waterless places, the basis of a demonology for which he is to be held responsible. (418)

As to William Tell, although I know that some critics now doubt whether he ever existed, when I hear a speaker mention something that he did, I always think that he believes the incident which he mentions, unless he gives some intimation to the contrary. If he introduces it as something that is *said* to have been done by William Tell, I understand him as doubting the story. As for Effie Deans, and the Man Without a Country, I confess myself so ignorant of them, that if I were to hear Professor Thayer in sober discourse mention something that either of them did, I would suppose that he was mentioning a real transaction. I stand with reference to William Tell where the Jews stood with reference to Jonah; and with reference to Effie Deans and the Man Without a Country, I stand as the Jews would have stood if they had never heard of Jonah. Jesus, then, if he did not believe the story of Jonah, would have made the same false impression on the Jews as the Professor would on me in the case of Effie Deans.

As to our Lord's remark about evil spirits frequenting waterless places, while it would be hazardous to make it the "basis of a demonology for which he is to be held responsible," he certainly is to be held responsible for the remark itself. If an evil spirit, when he left a man, did not frequent waterless places, I should be glad to learn from Professor Thayer what kind of places he did frequent. If we may judge by those that went into the herd of swine, the evil spirits were not fond of being in the water; and even before they went out of the man they kept him among the tombs, which were certainly waterless places. If, then, the statement about the evil spirit is to be taken as a parallel to that about Jonah, we should conclude that the latter was really three days and three nights in the fish. Moreover, if Jesus knew the mysterious movements of disembodied spirits, we might credit him with knowing something about men in the flesh like Jonah.

Professor Franklin Johnson, of Chicago University, makes the same argument with different illustrations:

> The great writers and orators of all peoples and ages have spoken of

> the characters of fiction as if they were real. All competent writers and orators do so today. Even the minister who is offended with these lines will refer in next Sunday's sermon to the prodigal son, to the sower, to the merchant seeking goodly pearls, without telling his people these characters are not historical. He will refer to Mr. Facing-both-ways, to Mr. Fearing, or to Christian at the Wicket Gate, in the Slough of Despond, or in the Vanity Fair, and will tell what they did, with no thought of the question whether his statements are derived from history or from allegory, I could show by many examples that this was the custom of the writers and speakers of antiquity. In fact, one of these examples is given by Christ himself. After relating the parable of the Unjust Judge, he begins his comment upon it with a sentence such as he would have used had the parable been history: "Hear what the unjust judge saith" (Luke 18.6). So also in Jude 7, 14, 15, the lord's brother refers to the story of the crime of the angels with the women of the world before the flood, without raising the question of its historical character, and quotes from the Book of Enoch, as we quote from some disputed dialogue of Plato, without raising the question of its genuineness. (418–419)

The Professor need not have insisted so earnestly that writers and orators of all peoples and ages speak of the characters of fiction as if they were real; for this is not denied by anybody. The question at issue is *evaded* by all such remarks, and by all the illustrations adduced in their support. The real question is, whether, in the specific remark of Christ about Jonah, and in strictly parallel remarks, the reality of the alleged experience is affirmed. This depends on the remark itself, and on the connection in which it occurs; but not on one or a thousand remarks of a different nature about other matters. Professor Johnson doubtless thought, when he wrote his article, that his examples were relevant and conclusive. Let us examine them, and see.

His first group includes three characters in the Saviour's parables; and he assumes that the prodigal son, the sower, and the dealer in pearls were not historical characters. How does he know that they were not? Did no sower ever go out to sow, and meet with the exact experience of the one in the parable? The Professor must know that this was the experience of thousands of sowers in

Palestine every year; and that it is to this day. Did no younger son ever pass through the identical experiences of the prodigal? Who can say no, when thousands of them are now passing through experiences almost identical? And as to the unjust judge, tyrannical governments in the East have swarmed with such in all ages, and no man can safely deny that one of them spoke and acted precisely as Jesus describes him. The second group of examples, taken from *Pilgrim's Progress,* can be used as they are for the reason, first, that nearly all auditors are familiar with them as fictitious characters; and second, because their very names are suggestive of fiction, and would be so understood on hearing them the first time. There is no parallel between them and the case in hand; for, in order to such a parallel the hearers of Jesus should have known that Jonah was a fictitious character, or else the language of Jesus should have been suggestive of fiction. In the third group, taken from Jude, the Professor assumes as correct an interpretation which is disputed; and even so he does not make good his point. The great majority of scholars deny that Jude makes any allusion to crime committed by angels with women; and if it can be made out that he does, then it will still be necessary, before the argument is made good, to show that the fact which be alludes to was not a fact; and this Professor Johnson can not do. He can make it appear very improbable, but further than this he can not go. On the contrary, if he could prove that Jude asserts that this crime was committed, he would thereby prove to most men that it really was. The case would then be like that of Jesus and Jonah. As to the Book of Enoch, Jude makes no statement on its authority. He makes a statement about Enoch which is also found substantially in that book; but he states it as a fact without referring to his source of knowledge, and nearly all men, since his epistle was written, have received it as a fact; so that, if it is not a fact, Jude has deceived them. This is a true parallel to the remark of Jesus about Jonah; for in both instances a fact is asserted, and men in general have believed the fact because of these assertions. Careful and elaborate, therefore, as is the argument of Professor Johnson, it is a failure.

Professor Hyde, the writer who thinks that the passage under consideration may mean "any one of ten thousands things to as many readers," and that "precisely what Jesus meant by it we shall never know," follows the same line of argument, and expresses himself thus:

> As to Jesus' use of the Old Testament, it seems to me that he used it just as we use Bunyan or Shakespeare—without concerning himself one way or the other about its historicity or literary form or authorship, or date of composition, and assuming that his immediate hearers would have sufficient common sense to take his words as he meant them. To tie him down to a belief in the historical character of the story of Jonah is as absurd as it would be to make every man who ever referred to the Slough of Despond a believer in the geographical reality of such a place. (419–420)

If Jesus used the Old Testament as we use Bunyan and Shakespeare, he used it as an allegory or a poem, and in no sense as history. It is astonishing that a sane man can so assert or believe. But Perhaps the Professor intended to qualify the statement by the words, "without concerning himself one way or the other about its historicity or literary form or authorship, or date of composition." But if he used it without concerning himself about its historicity or its authorship, he did not use it as we use Bunyan and Shakespeare. Who quotes either of these authors without concerning himself about their historicity? The man who would use Anthony's oration over Caesar's dead body, or Christian's struggle through the Slough of Despond, as a piece of history, would be set down as an ignoramus or deceiver; and the man who would quote Shakespeare in the name of Milton, or Bunyan in the name of Ben Jonson would reap the same reward. We do not then use these two works, or any other worlds, without concerning ourselves about their historicity or their authorship; and the same is true of Jesus in his dealings with the Old Testament. The Professor's citation of the Slough of Despond is wide of the mark; for the only reason why a public speaker can now refer to that without misleading his hearers into the belief of its reality, is that his hearers already know it to be an imaginary slough. If the hearers of Jesus had so understood the story of Jonah, the cases would be parallel; but it is notorious, and it is freely admitted that they understood the story to be true, and when, therefore, Jesus spoke of it as a true story he deceived them if it was not. This point, let me say with emphasis, is totally ignored by all the writers on the side with these eight. Why so? Is it because they are too dull to see that such a point can be made in answer to them? I can not think so. Why, then, do they ignore it? I should be glad to know. I hope I shall obtain from some of them an answer.

The fifth writer in the symposium is Philip S. Moxom, of Springfield, Mass. As he denies the genuineness of the passage under consideration, he saves himself the necessity of trying to prove that the remark of Jesus about Jonah does not imply the reality of Jonah's experience; we therefore pass on to the sixth writer, who is Professor Rhees, of Newton Theological Institution. He says:

> It is evident that in Jesus' words the story of Jonah is treated as historical. The contemporaries of Jesus held it to be sober history. And Jonah is appealed to in the same way as Abraham and David are referred to in the New Testament. It is to be noticed, however, that the reference is only by way of *illustration*. And consequently it may not be said that the validity of the illustration passes, if the story is found to be allegory and not fullest history. So long as it served to suggest to the hearers of Jesus the thought of his vindication by a miraculous deliverance, the story would be an apt illustration. And we need not doubt that our Lord would use it without raising the question of its historicity. (425–426)

This writer, like all the others, evades the real issue and raises another. The question is not, whether an illustration drawn from a supposed fact would be invalidated by the discovery that the account of the fact is allegorical; but whether the particular use that Jesus made of the story of Jonah implies that Jonah was in the fish. When Prof. Rhees says, at the beginning of the extract just made, that in the words of Jesus the story of Jonah is treated as historical, and adds that the contemporaries of Jesus held it to be sober history, he cuts himself off from all escape in the direction in which he seeks it; for if Jesus treated the story as historical in speaking to men who held it to be so, then he was either mistaken about it himself, or he deceived his hearers. There is no possible escape from this alternative.

To say that the reference to Jonah is "only by way of illustration," betrays still greater confusion of thought. What was he aiming to illustrate? Let us try a strictly parallel remark: "As in Adam all die, so also in Christ shall all be made alive." Is this an illustration? To ask the question is to answer it. Instead of being an illustration, it is the prediction of a future fact and the declaration that it will be as universal as a well-known fact in the past. The undoubted reality of the past fact is what gives force to the assertion respecting the future one. If a man could answer Paul by saying, Very well; all did *not* die in Adam; he could add, Then all, according to your own showing, will *not* be made alive in Christ. So in the present instance. If the Pharisees could have answered Jesus, as these critics now do, by saying, Very well, Master; Jonah was not in the bowels of the fish; they could have added, Therefore, according to your own showing, you will not be in the heart of the earth. Instead of being an illustration of something,—and Professor Rhees does not attempt to tell us of what—the remark was a solemn prediction of a fact yet to be, which should be analogous to one that certainly had been.

But Professor Rhees, like all the others of the symposium, presents a supposed parallel to the remark in question, by which he attempts to sustain his interpretation. He says:

> It is not generally held that by his words in the parable of the rich man and Lazarus, Jesus has given sanction to the feature of Jewish eschatology which pictured the blessed dead, in waiting for the resurrection, as reclining in Abraham's bosom. It is no more necessary to hold that he has here sanctioned any particular conclusion concerning the nature of the narrative in the Book of Jonah. (426)

If there was any such "feature of Jewish eschatology" as is here intimated, I am sure Jesus never uttered a word to give sanction to it. It would have been too foolish a "feature" for any thoughtful man to sanction; for how could all the millions of the "blessed dead" recline in the bosom of a single man? This "feature" would require Abraham to have an enormous bosom. It was a kindred thought, perhaps, which caused the men who constructed the grave of Noah, which is pointed out to the traveler in Palestine, to make it *ninety feet long.* No, Professor; Jesus did not sanction so absurd a "feature"; but he did say that angels bore *Lazarus* into Abraham's bosom; and I don't know any more comfortable place to which they could have borne him. There was room enough for *him* in the bosom of the patriarch, and if Professor Rhees does not believe that he was really borne thither, will he please to tell us whither he was borne? I know so little about that region myself, that I can take Jesus at his word when he speaks of it. If I reject his word about it, to whom shall I go?

The next writer, Amory H. Bradford, expresses himself very briefly and very clearly. He says:

> If the Book of Jonah was known by the Master to be a parable written for the purpose of conveying a great moral lesson, he might have referred to it in the language here used. He would not have conveyed a false impression, since his hearers would have understood his reference. (427)

This last remark shows that Mr. Bradford has caught one idea which the other writers have missed. He sees that, in order to avoid making a false impression by referring to an imaginary fact as if it were real, the hearers as well as the speaker must understand the reference. But while he is undoubtedly correct in this he forgets that if Jesus made such a reference as this, his hearers did *not* understand the reference, for it is admitted on all hands that the Jews understood the story of Jonah to be sober history; and if Jesus did not so understand it, then, according to Mr. Bradford's own showing, he made a false impression. This writer has stumbled on the truth at one point, only to stumble over it at another.

Like the others, this writer finds a parallel, as he supposes, in an admissible use of fictitious characters, and his chosen example is taken from the novel, *Les Miserables:*

> Preachers not infrequently refer to the good bishop in *Les Miserables* as if he were a historical person; but because Canon Stubbs speaks of that story as if it were true, no one thinks that he means to be so

> understood, and if it is not true he can never be trusted again. He took it for granted that his hearers understood him and did not need to qualify his statement. It is quite conceivable that our Lord spoke in the same way. (427)

Very well; Canon Stubbs took it for granted that his hearers understood him as not affirming the truth of the story of the bishop, but in the case of Jesus the reverse was true; so the cases are not parallel. If Canon Stubbs would have misled his hearers, had they *not* understood him as they did, then Jesus misled his hearers if he understood the story of Jonah to be fictitious. Mr. Bradford must wipe out all that he has written in this symposium and make a new start from a different point of view, if he is to maintain his contention.

Near the close of his brief article, Mr. Bradford takes another turn in his effort to get rid of the natural view of the case. He says:

> He was not asked about the story; he as asked for a sign, and his reference to Jonah was incidental, and used because it would be easily understood by those whom he addressed. (428)

Yes; "easily understood by those whom he addressed"; and understood, as we have again and again reiterated, as a *real event.* Being so understood by them, we ask again, How can Jesus be relieved of the charge of duplicity if he knew that the event was not real, and yet used it to confirm their impression that it was? Again I demand that some of the critics shall answer this question.

As Professor Ropes, the last of the eight, denies that Jesus knew any more about the Book of Jonah than did his contemporaries, he, of course, is freed from the necessity of explaining how he could consistently refer to the incident of the fish as a reality when it was not. He did so, according to this Professor, because he knew no better than to believe the story.

We now come to the comments made on this symposium by the associate editor of the *Biblical World.* Professor Shailer Mathews. He states the common belief of the eight writers in these words:

> Christ's use of the experience of Jonah as an illustration, in no way gives his sanction to the view that the Book of Jonah is history.

In this attempt to represent the common belief of the writers, the editor has drawn up on his imagination rather than upon the articles of the writers; for only one of them says that Jesus used the experience of Jonah as an *illustration;* and I have showed very plainly, I think, that he did not so use it.

These writers all feel, at least those of them who credit Jesus with knowing the facts about Jonah, that the only way to defend their position is to find, either in the lips of Jesus himself, or in those of some other approved speaker, a parallel statement in which the reality of the past fact referred to is not implied. They have ransacked the writings of Shakespeare, of Bunyan, of the popular novelists, and the parables of Jesus, to find one, and they have brought forth many; but every one of them fails, as we have seen, in the essential point of comparison. Let them find, if they can, a single instance in which Jesus mentioned something in the past which his hearers believed to be a fact, but which he certainly knew to be not a fact, and then compared with this some event yet in the future. I have given one allusion that is parallel, the saying of Paul, "As in Adam all die, so in Christ shall all be made alive"; but the allusion is to a real past event. Here is another example: "This Jesus, who was received up from you into heaven, shall so come in like manner as ye beheld him going into heaven" (Acts 1.11). Here the past event, his going into heaven, was a real one. Again: "As therefore the tares are gathered up and burned with fire, so shall it be in the end of the world. The Son of man shall send forth his angels, and they shall gather out of his kingdom all things that cause stumbling, and them that do iniquity, and shall cast them into the furnace of fire" (Matt 13.40–41). Here is a strictly parallel case, and the past event, the gathering and burning of the tares, is strictly historical. "As Moses lifted up the serpent in the wilderness, so the Son of man must be lifted up" (John 3.14). Again: "As it came to pass in the days of Noah, even so shall it be also in the days of the Son of man" (Luke 12.26). I know not how many more instances of the same construction can be found, for I have mentioned these only from memory; but let the critics find at least one such in which the past event, though spoken of as a reality, and believed by the hearer to be a reality, was known by Jesus to be a fiction. Then, and not till then, may they claim that the story of Jonah may also be a fiction, notwithstanding the use Jesus makes of it. If he had said, As the trees went forth once to choose for themselves a king, so shall something else yet take place; and had the Jews believed that Jothan's fable was a piece of history, this would be such an example as the critics are searching for. Again, I say, let them find such an example, and cease their endless production of parallels that are not parallels. I am neither a prophet, nor the son of a prophet, but I stake my reputation as a man of some knowledge of the subject on the assertion that the example demanded will never be found.

2. Professor Driver on the Book of Jonah

I propose next to review the new critical theory as to the origin and character of the Book of Jonah. I select, as representing most fairly that theory, what Professor Driver says in his *Introduction to the Literature of the Old Testament.*

No author whom I have read has a better conception of the design of the book; for as an exegete, Professor Driver has few superiors; but on the question of historicity he stands with the scholars whose symposium I have reviewed, and he assigns to the book a date so late as to render its historicity a matter of impossibility, unless its author was miraculously inspired to know the history, which he tacitly denies.

I will state his position in his own words, and then consider *seriatim* the reasons by which he supports it. He says:

> On the historical character of the narrative opinions have differed widely. Quite irrespectively of the miraculous features in the narrative it must be admitted that there are indications that it is not strictly historical.

The first of these "indications" which he mentions is set forth as follows:

> The sudden conversion on such a large scale as (without pressing single expressions) is evidently implied, of a great heathen population is contrary to analogy; nor is it easy to imagine a monarch of the type depicted in the Assyrian inscriptions behaving as the king of Nineveh is represented as acting in the presence of the Hebrew prophet. (p. 303)

According to this mode of reasoning, an account of any sudden change in a great population, which is "contrary to analogy," is to be regarded as self-evidently unhistorical; and if one in a succession of kings is represented as acting a much humbler part than the others, it is difficult to imagine that the representation is true. I wonder, then, what Professor Driver thinks of the statement, contrary to all analogy, that three thousand persons were converted to Christ by a single discourse of Peter on the great Pentecost? And what does he think of the account of Sergius Paulus, who is said, contrary to the analogy of Roman Proconsuls, to have suddenly believed in Jesus after a brief interview with Paul and Barnabas? What does he think of the great waves of religious revolutions, quite similar to that on Pentecost, which have often characterized modern revivals in both Christian and heathen lands? Such reasoning would destroy all faith in the most striking events of history. But the critics of this new school, like the avowed enemies of the Bible, never reason thus except when they are seeking to set aside the historicity of some Bible narrative. Their antipathy to the belief of events that are contrary to analogy seem limited to Biblical events.

The author's second reason is given in these words:

> It is remarkable, also, that the conversion of Nineveh, if it took place upon the scale described should have produced so little permanent effect; for the Assyrians are uniformly represented in the Old Testament as idolaters.

Is it not equally remarkable that the frequent conversions of Israel under the Judges should have had so little permanent effect? That the conversion of Judah under Hezekiah should have had so little permanent effect as to be followed immediately by the abominable idolatries of Manasseh's reign? Paul marveled that the Galatians had so soon turned away from him who called them, to another gospel—a backward revolution in less than three years; yet, all these things, remarkable as they were, actually took place. Is an account of something "remarkable" to be understood as indicating that the book containing it is not historical? If so, we must scout all history except that of the most commonplace character. The school to which Professor Driver belongs deals thus, I say again, only with the narratives of the Bible. And this mode of treatment is in the present instance the more remarkable from the consideration that although it is true that the Ninevites are represented in the Old Testament, when their religion is mentioned at all, as idolaters, they are not mentioned after the visit of Jonah till the reign of Pul, King of Assyria, who made a friendly alliance with Menahem, of Israel. Now Menahem came to the throne two years after the death of Jeroboam, and he had been reigning some years when Pul marched across the Euphrates; and if the visit of Jonah to Nineveh occurred some years before the death of Jeroboam, then we have a lapse of from five or six to a dozen or more years before Nineveh is mentioned again; and even then it is only her king who is mentioned, without a word as to the religious condition of her people. Now if Jonah did not believe that the repentance of the Ninevites would last through forty days, should it be considered very "remarkable" that we have no trace of it after a few years?

The third reason given by Professor Driver is more remarkable still. It is this:

> But in fact the structure of the narrative shows that the *didactic purpose* of the book is the author's chief aim. He introduces just those details that have a bearing upon this, while omitting others which, had his interest been in the history as such, might naturally have been mentioned; *e.g.*, details as to the spot at which Jonah was cast on the island, and particulars as to the special sins of which the Ninevites were guilty.

I wonder what man of sense ever attempted to write history with an "interest in the history as such," and without a *didactic* aim as his chief purpose in writing. Surely, no such historical writing can be found in the Bible. Even the four Gospels, though devoted to the most deeply interesting historical events that ever transpired on this old earth, had a *didactic* purpose as their chief aim—the purpose, as John expresses it, of causing the readers to believe that Jesus is the Christ, the Son of the living God, and that believing they might obtain life through his name. History is said to be philosophy teaching by example; and if a narrative teaches nothing, if it has not a didactic purpose as its chief aim, then it is not history according to the accepted definition. And what wonderful omissions the author of the Book of Jonah was led to make by his didactic purpose! He failed to tell the exact spot where Jonah was thrown up; and what a loss to the modern tourist! I wonder if Jonah himself knew where he was thrown up. I wonder if he ever went back and tried to identify it. Surely, for the benefit of modern critics, he ought to have driven a stake there, or built a heap of stones; for why should the world be deprived of information so necessary to its spiritual welfare? And then, be omitted to mention the special sins of which the Ninevites were guilty! True, everybody knew them, and every intelligent person knows now the sins to which idolatrous cities have been most addicted; but surely, if the author of Jonah had been a modern critic of the school of Driver, he would not have been so absorbed in his didactic purpose as to omit this needed information!

After giving all these reasons for believing that the narrative in question is not "strictly historical," the author, on the same page, and in the very next paragraph makes the following statement:

> No doubt the materials of the narrative were supplied to the author by tradition, and rest ultimately upon a basis of fact; no doubt the outlines of the narrative are historical, and Jonah's preaching was actually successful at Nineveh (Luke 11.30–32), though not upon the scale represented in the book.

"No doubt" on the points here mentioned? "No doubt" that the narrative rests upon a basis of fact? "No doubt" that the outlines of the narrative are historical? "No doubt" that Jonah's preaching was actually successful at Nineveh? Why no doubt on these points, when everything else in the book is doubted or denied? If the author invented the fish story, and the gourd story, and the universal repentance of the Ninevites, why is there no doubt that he told the truth about the other details? There is nothing in the book itself to indicate such a difference, and there is nothing in contemporary history. Where, then, does Professor Driver obtain the conviction, free from all doubt, that so much of the story is true? The only clue that he gives us in his very quiet citation of Luke 11.30–32. And what is found there? Why, those very statements of Jesus which the eight scholars in our symposium will not allow to have any bearing on the historical character of the Book of Jonah. We there find the words, "For even as Jonah was a sign to the Ninevites, so shall also the Son of man be to this generation." "The men of Nineveh shall stand up in the judgment with this generation, and shall condemn it: for they repented at the preaching of Jonah; and behold, a greater than Jonah is here." Professor Driver, then, stands against our chosen eight on this point; for he affirms what they deny, that the statement of Jesus proves the historicity of the Book of Jonah in the particulars mentioned, that is, his being a sign to the Ninevites, and the repentance of the latter under his preaching. With him there is "no doubt" on these points. But right here there springs up a very serious question, to which Professor Driver ought to give a very serious answer. If the words of Jesus, to which he refers, prove that the narrative of Jonah rests "ultimately upon a basis of fact"; that the outlines of the narrative are historical, and that the Ninevites did actually repent, why does not his explicit declaration that "Jonah was three days and three nights in the bowels of the sea monster" prove that this also is historical? I am afraid, after all, that the ultimate reason for denying the credibility of the narrative is that which is the avowed reason of unbelievers—an unwillingness to accept the miraculous in the story—and this is the very essence of skepticism. That the kind of criticism in which Professor Driver and all belonging to the same school indulge, is incipient unbelief, becomes more and more apparent the more closely it is scrutinized, and the further its development progresses.

Further on I propose to review Professor Driver's evidence for the late date of the Book of Jonah; but under heading he has an argument which more properly belongs to the subject now before me, and I will notice it here. It is expressed thus:

> The non-mention of the name of the king of Nineveh, who plays such a prominent part in chapter three, may be taken as an implication that it was not known to the author of the book. (p. 301)

If the name of the king was not known to the author of the book, then of course, the author was not Jonah; neither was he one who had obtained full information from Jonah; but is the book, therefore, unhistorical? I can imagine an author who had learned correctly every detail except the king's name. It seems to me that the "non-mention" of the king's name has no bearing on the question either way; for if Jonah wrote it, his didactic purpose depended upon the *repentance* of the king, and not upon his *name;* and if a romancer of the fifth century BC wrote it, he could just as easily have invented the name of the king as to have invented as he is supposed to have done, the story of the fish and that of the gourd vine. The Book of Judith is a romance of about the character ascribed by our critics to the Book of Jonah; and the author of it does not hesitate to give the name of the imaginary Holofernes whose imaginary head the imaginary Judith cut off; then why should the author of the Book of Jonah, while manufacturing much of the story, have hesitated to put in the name of the king, whether he knew it or not?

It is the custom of destructive critics to assign dates to the historical books of the Bible so far this side of the events as to render it impossible for their authors to have had accurate information. This they have done, not only with Old Testament books, but with the Gospels and Acts; and this they have done with the Book of Jonah. Following their lead, Professor Driver and the less destructive school to which he belongs, have selected the fifth century BC as the date of this book; and as Jonah lived near the close of the ninth century, this leaves an interval of nearly four hundred years between the composition of the book and the events of his life. This would make no difference in case of the real inspiration of the author; but these critics grant to Bible writers no inspiration which could bring to their knowledge forgotten facts of the past, or that could guard them against errors in recording facts. So then it becomes us to examine the grounds on which so late a date is assigned to this book.

The first evidence given by Driver is based upon the alleged use by the author of Aramaic words and forms, which did not come into use until the Babylonian captivity. After saying that the book can not have been written till long after the lifetime of Jonah himself, he adds: "This appears, (1) from the style, which has several Aramaisms, or other marks of a late age"; and he proceeds to specify a half dozen such words. I will not copy these and comment on them, seeing that the author himself almost immediately admits that there is nothing conclusive in the evidence.

He says in the next paragraph:

> Some of the linguistic features might (possibly) be consistent with a preëxilic origin in Northern Israel (though they are more pronounced than those referred to page 177n): but taken as a whole, they are more naturally explained by the supposition that the book is a work of the post-exilic period, to which other considerations point with some cogency.

This is what a musician would style playing *diminuendo*. The confident assertion that the writing "has several Aramaisms," is followed by the admission that these may possibly be consistent with the early origin of the book, and this reduces the conclusion to a mere possibility.

I now quote the second evidence:

> (2) From the Psalm in chapter two, which consists largely of reminiscences from Psalms (in the manner of Psa 142, 143, 144.1–11), many of them not of early origin (compare verse 2, Psalms 18, 65, 120, 1; verse 3, Psa 18, 4, 42, 7; verse 4, Psa 31, 22, Lam 3, Psa 54; verse 5, Psa 18, 4, 116, 3, 69, 1; verse 6, Psa 30, 3; verse 7, Psa 142, 3, 18, 6; verse 8, Psa 31, 6; verse 9, Psa 50, 14, 116, 17, 3, 8): a Psalm of Jonah's own age would certainly have been more original as it would also have shown a more antique coloring.

Lest the reader should fail to look up these references, and to make the comparisons necessary in order to see the force of the evidence, I shall copy the passages referred to in full. I shall do this for another reason—because it is quite the custom of these critics to present an array of references which scarcely anybody will have the patience to study out, but which will be taken by many as conclusive proof that the learned and laborious author has by hard labor learned the absolute truth of what he is writing.

A severe test of some of these groups of figures now and then is a healthy exercise for the reader and it often proves a bombshell under the writer. Below I give the verses in Jonah's psalm cited above, and those in other psalms of which it is claimed that they are reminiscences.

Verse 2

"I cried by reason of mine affliction unto the Lord,
And he answered me;
Out of the belly of Sheol cried I,
And thou heardest my voice."

Alleged Parallels

"The chords of Sheol were round about me:
The snares of death came upon me.
In my distress I called upon the Lord,
And cried unto my God:
He heard my voice out of his temple,
And my cry before him came into his ears." (Psa 18.5–6)

"In my distress I cried unto the Lord,
And he answered me." (Psa 120.1)

Now, the only thoughts common to these passages are those of calling upon, or crying to God in distress, and being heard by him; and these are so commonplace in the experiences of praying people, that to find them expressed in similar terms by different authors, is no evidence at all that one copies from another.

Verse 3

"For thou didst cast me into the deep, in the heart of the seas,
And the flood was round about me;
All thy waves and thy billows passed over me."

Alleged Parallels

"And the floods of ungodliness made me afraid." (Psa 18.4)
"Deep calleth unto deep at the noise of thy water-spouts:

All thy waves and thy billows are gone over me." (Psa 42.7)

The only identical thought common to any two of these three passages, is that respecting God's waves and billows; and there is no ground for assuming that in either there is a reminiscence from the other. In the latter instance the writer is speaking figuratively of his troubles, which he compares to waves and billows going over him, a very common comparison for one living by the sea; and Jonah, when in the fish's bowels, had no reason to remember the psalm in order to say that the waves and billows were rolling over him.

Verse 4
"And I said, I am cast out from before thine eyes;
Yet I will look again toward thy holy temple."

Alleged Parallels
"As for me, I said in my haste, I am cut off from before thine eyes.
Nevertheless thou heardest the voice of my supplication when I cried unto thee." (Psa 31.22)

"Waters flowed over my head: I said I am cut off." (Lam 3.54)

The idea of being "cut off," when in great trouble, is the only one common to these passages; but surely it is, too commonplace to justify the assumption of a reminiscence. It occurs dozens of times in the Old Testament, as any one can see by a mere glance at a Concordance.

Verse 5
"The waters compassed me about, even to the soul;
The deep was round about me:
The weeds were wrapped about my head."

Alleged Parallels
"The cords of death compassed me
And the floods of ungodliness made me afraid." (Psa 18.4)

"The cords of death compassed me,
And the pains of Sheol got hold upon me:
I found trouble and sorrow." (Psa 116.3)

"Save me, O God:
For the waters are come in unto my soul." (Psa 20.1)

While we have here a striking reminiscence in one of the psalms from the other, the only appearance of reminiscence between either and Jonah is, found in the clauses, "The waters are come *in unto my soul,*" and, "the waters compassed me about *even to the soul.*" This is very probably a reminiscence; for the thought of waters, either real, or figuratively so-called, so pressing around one as to reach his soul, is quite original, and is not likely to have originated with two writers independently. But if David wrote the Sixty-ninth Psalm, as its inscription asserts, or if it was written by any one who lived between David and Jonah, then a reminiscence from it in the Book of Jonah does not prove a date for the latter this side the prophet's own lifetime. To serve the purpose of our critic, it must be proved that the psalm was written too late for the author of the Book of Jonah to have seen it, and, at the same time, to have had authentic knowledge of Jonah's career. This can not be done.

Verse 6

"I went down to the bottom of the mountains;
The earth with her bars closed upon me forever:
Yet hast thou brought up my life from the pit,
O Lord my God."

Alleged Parallel

"O Lord, thou hast brought up my soul from Sheol:
Thou hast kept me alive, that I should not go down to the pit."
(Psa 30.3)

Here everything turns upon the use of the word pit. To go down to the pit is a common expression in many Old Testament writers (see Concordance) for death; and to fall into a pit, for any sudden calamity. When, therefore, it is said by Jonah, "Thou hast brought up my life from the pit," he was using a commonplace figure of speech, but reversing the direction of the thought, as his deliverance from death required. Instead of a reminiscence from the Thirtieth Psalm, there is here only the use of an expression very common among his countrymen.

Verse 7

"When my soul fainted within me, I remembered the Lord:
And my prayer came in unto thee, into thy holy temple."

Alleged Parallels

"When my soul fainted within me thou knewest my path.
In the way wherein I walked have they hidden a snare for me." (Psa 142.3)

"In my distress I called upon the name of the Lord,
And cried unto my God;
He heard my voice out of his temple,
And my cry came before him into his ears." (Psa 18.6)

Here we have the identical expression, "My soul fainted within me," and the identical thought that the prayer of the man in distress came in unto the Lord; but both the expression and the thought are commonplace, and give no evidence that the author of either poem had seen the other.

Verse 8

"They that regard lying vanities,
Forsake their own mercy."

Alleged Parallel

"I hate them that regard lying vanities;
But I trust in the Lord." (Ps 31.6)

The term vanities occurs a number of times in the Old Testament, being found in Deuteronomy (32.21), 1 Kings (16.13, 26), and in other books; but the expression "lying vanities" is found only in these two places, and it is probably a reminiscence in one or the other. If the psalm, as its superscription asserts, was written by David, the author of Jonah may have borrowed the expression from it; but if the psalm was written after the captivity, then the author of it may have borrowed from Jonah.

Verse 9

"But I will sacrifice unto thee with the voice of thanksgiving,
I will pay that which I have vowed.
Salvation is of the Lord."

Alleged Parallels

"Offer unto God the sacrifices of thanksgiving;
And pay the vows unto the Most High." (Psa 50.14)

"I will offer unto thee sacrifices of thanksgiving,
And will call upon the name of the Lord." (Psa 116.17)

"Salvation belongeth unto the Lord;
Thy blessing be upon thy people." (Psa 3.8)

In the identical expression, "sacrifice of thanksgiving," found in the two psalms, there is undoubtedly a reminiscence; but the expression is found in the Book of Leviticus, where it occurs repeatedly (see Lev 7.12–13; 22.29), and this book was written, according to the received chronology, more than five hundred years before the time of Jonah. But as this does not suit our critics, who deny the Mosaic authorship of Leviticus, we must tell them that it also occurs in the Book of Amos, who, as they all admit, was a contemporary of Jonah. Amos says to Israel: "Offer a sacrifice of thanksgiving of that which is leavened; and proclaim free-will offerings, and publish them" (4.5). If, then, it is a reminiscence in Jonah, it could have been taken from Amos, and it is idle to claim that it was taken from psalms written four hundred years later. But after all, the author of Jonah does not use the exact expression, or express the exact idea found in Amos, in the law, and in the Psalms; for his words are not, "I will offer the sacrifices of thanksgiving"; but, "I will sacrifice unto thee with the voice of thanksgiving."

As to the thought expressed at the close of verse 9, "Salvation is of the Lord"; and in the Third Psalm, "Salvation belongeth unto the Lord"; it is expressed so often in nearly the same words, and is a thought so commonplace in itself, that it furnished no evidence of a reminiscence.

We have now gone over this whole formidable list of "reminiscences, and we have found only two or three of them which call with any plausibility be so called. It is easy to see that the critic who compiled it took up every verse, and every clause of every verse in the poem of Jonah, and with Concordance in hand ransacked all the Psalms which he supposed of late date, together with other late writings, in search of words, phrases, and thoughts, which he could say were borrowed from these by the author of Jonah. This is a very cheap show of learning; for a boy twelve years old could do the work. The result is the empty basket which we have just turned bottom upward.

If the attempt had been a success, we should have found every single sentence in this beautiful poem of Jonah a borrowed scrap from the pen of some real poet, and the whole would have been a "patch quilt," without a piece of original goods to be seen. I venture the assertion that so excellent a poem as this was never composed in this way since the world began; and it never will be. On the contrary, it would be most natural for poets writing at a later day, and being perfectly familiar with this poem to borrow, some one, and some another, of its fine passages, and use them in their own compositions. But natural as this is, it was not done except in two or three instances at most, and these we have pointed out above.

3. Is the Story of Jonah Incredible?

If I were to hear the naked statement, without preface or supplement, that a man was once thrown overboard from a ship, was swallowed by a fish as he fell into the sea, was kept in the fish's bowels three days and three nights alive, and then thrown up alive on dry land, I would regard it as a "fish story," and pay no attention to it. So, if I were to hear the naked story that a man once went into the greatest and wickedest city on the earth, and by preaching against it one day caused the people, from the king on his throne to the beggar on the street, to sit down in sack-cloth and ashes and call mightily on God till he heard and forgave then, I would think of the life-long preaching done by Spurgeon in London, and that of other great preachers in other great cities, and I would not believe the story. Again, if I were to hear, without historical connections, that a man was sitting once on a sandhill in a very hot country, suffering almost death with the heat, and that in a single night a gourdvine grew up, and the next day made a delightful shade over his head, I would think of Jack and the Bean Stalk, and would treat it as an idle tale. In like manner, here I to hear that a man once stood at the mouth of a cave, and called to a dead man within, who had been dead four days, and that the dead man immediately stood outside the cave alive, still bound hand and foot with the grave cloths, I would not believe that till I learned who did it, and why it was done.

Now unfortunately this is the way in which the three principal incidents in the story of Jonah come to the ears of many persons, and it accounts for the widespread incredulity respecting them.

To believe them is to believe three miracles; and we can not believe that a mere idle wonder is a work of God's hand. A year or two ago I went to see the performance of Herrmann, the great magician; and I witnessed feats that were as mysterious to me as any miracles of which we read in the Bible; but if Herrmann had claimed, which he did not, that they were wrought by the direct power of God, I would have denied it flatly; for I could not believe that God would take part in a show which did no good except to gratify idle curiosity, and to fill Herrmann's pocket with silver. If I am called on to believe a wonder which could be wrought only by the direct power of God, I must see in it something that makes it worthy of God. When the occasion is such, or the manifest purpose is such, as to demand, or even to justify, the interposition of God's hand, this at once removes the incredibility which would otherwise attach to the story. I propose now to look at the story of Jonah from this point of view, and to see if it will remain incredible after it is understood.

Behold, then, the city of Nineveh, "that great city," the greatest that had thus far been built on earth, the head of the Assyrian Empire, which was the greatest and most powerful empire yet established among men. The city is wholly given to idolatry, and to all those abominations which ever characterize idolatrous peoples. It leads in these abominations all the nations of Western Asia, over all of which its king has rule. God looks down upon the vast population of both city and empire, and he sees in every individual of the teeming millions one of the immortal creatures of his hand reveling in iniquity and rushing on to eternal ruin. He is the same God who so loved the world that he gave his own Son, that whosoever believeth in him might not perish, but have eternal life. Did he who cared so much for men afterward, care nothing for them then? Or, do not the words just quoted express the divine compassion which moved him in all the ages before the advent of Christ? He longs for these prodigals, and he is about to institute measures to bring them to repentance.

The Scriptures reveal to us no way in which God brings men to repentance, except in connection with preaching. But if Nineveh is to be brought to repentance, the task must be assigned to no ordinary preacher. God assigned it to the prophet Jonah, the son of Amittai, of Gath-hepher. Very little is said of this prophet outside the book which bears his name, but that little implies a great deal. He lived under the reign of Jeroboam the Second. This prince came to the throne of Israel under most discouraging circumstances. During the reign of his grandfather, Jehoahaz, Hazael, king of Syria, had subdued and overrun Israel. In the expressive language of the Book of Kings, he "destroyed them, and made them like the dust in threshing." He left Jehoahaz only fifty horsemen, ten chariots and ten thousand footmen (2 Kgs 13.3–7). His son Joash, by three successful battles fought under encouragement given by the prophet Elisha, succeeded in throwing off the yoke of Syria, but the country was left in extreme weakness and distress, so that with reference to the beginning of Jeroboam's reign it is said: "The Lord saw the affliction of Israel, that it was very bitter; for there was none shut up or left at large, neither was there any helper for Israel" (14.26). Though coming to the throne under such circumstances, Jeroboam, in the course of a reign of forty-one years, not only re-established the prosperity of his nation, but he conquered Syria, and extended the northern boundary of his kingdom to the utmost limit that it had attained under David and Solomon. In the language of the text, "He restored the border of Israel from the entering of Hamath unto the sea of the Arabah [the Dead Sea]"; and he did this, the text adds, "according to the word of Jehovah, the God of Israel, which he spake by the hand of his servant Jonah, the son of Amittai, the prophet, which was of Gath-hepher" (14.25). The account of this long reign and of these mighty conquests is remarkably brief, being limited to *four verses;* but the author refers the reader for the "rest of the acts of Jeroboam, and all that he did, and his might, how he warred, and how he recovered Damascus, and Hamath," to the Book of the Chronicles of the Kings of Israel. Doubtless if we had that book we should find the story a long one.

Now if, in the absence of the fuller record, we inquire how it was that all these conquests were made "according to the word of Jehovah, the God of Israel, which he spake by the mouth of his servant Jonah," I think we shall find the answer in what the author tells us a few chapters back of a similar work done by the prophet Elisha. This famous prophet lived under the reign of Jehoram of Israel, who was continually at war with Ben-Hadad, king of Syria. During those wars the king of Syria frequently took counsel with his chief officers, and said: "In such and such a place shall be my camp." But Elisha would say to Jehoram: "Beware that thou pass not such a place, for thither the Syrians are coming down." By accepting this warning the king of Israel "saved himself, not once or twice," which means many times. It was impossible that the king of Syria should fail to see every time that his plans had been anticipated; so "his heart was sorely troubled about this thing." As his plans had been made known only to his confidential advisers, he came to the conclusion that one of them was betraying him. He called them together and demanded: "Will ye not show me which of us is for the king of Israel?" One of them promptly answered: "Nay, my lord, O king; but Elisha, the prophet that is in Israel, telleth the king of Israel the words that thou speakest in thy bedchamber" (2 Kgs 6.8–12). Ben-Hadad inquired where Elisha was sojourning, and sent a troop of cavalry to surround the town of Dothan and take him prisoner, with the result that Elisha took captive the whole troop, but gave them a good dinner and sent them home unharmed. Having given us this account, when the author says that the victories of Jeroboam were achieved according to the word of Jehovah by Jonah, he leaves us to suppose that the process was the same, of similar. We must understand, then, that during the forty-one years of Jeroboam's reign, Jonah was his prophetic adviser respecting his military movements, and that his fame as such was spread abroad among surrounding nations. Especially would it have spread into the region about Nineveh, which was separated from the field of Jeroboam's conquests only try the river Euphrates. It is very clear from all this that Jonah was the most famous, and the greatest prophet then living. It was in accord, therefore, with the wisdom which governs all of God's dealings with men, that he, rather than any other man, was selected to preach to the Ninevites.

There are times in the experience of every community, when rebukes from a preacher of righteousness fall unheeded on the ears of the people; and there are others, when the same rebukes are rewarded with the richest results. In our common experience we can learn in which of these conditions a community is only by trial; and we are often very bitterly disappointed. But God, who knows the secrets of all hearts, can never be mistaken in choosing the hour at which to strike, and he chose a favorable time at which to send Jonah to Nineveh. The history of the city at that particular time is to us wrapped in profound obscurity; and it is a fair inference that the empire was in a depressed condition, furnishing no startling events to catch the attention of historian or sculptor. Such a state of affairs would be favorable to a call for repentance. At the precise time in which the people were best prepared for such a message, God spoke to Jonah at his home in Gath-hepher, and said: "Arise, go to Nineveh, that great city, and cry against it; for their wickedness is come up before me" (Jon 1.1–2). Instead of obeying, Jonah arose and started in the opposite direction. God's command would have sent him toward the north, but he turns toward the south, and he stops not until he reaches Joppa, the principal seaport of the kingdom of Judah. Here he finds a ship sailing to Tarshish, the farthest port of the west to which vessels then sailed. He was running "away from the presence of Jehovah," which means from the region in which he thought it probable that Jehovah would speak to him again. He supposed that if he could get as far away as Tarshish, God would not call him back from so great a distance to send him on the disagreeable mission.

We might conjecture a number of motives for which Jonah undertook this desperate flight, and perhaps all of them might have had some part in causing it; for men do not often embark upon desperate enterprises without a number of motives; but there is one which he himself mentioned afterward, and we must accept this as at least the chief of all. When, afterward, he saw that God did not destroy the city according to his prediction, "it displeased Jonah exceedingly, and he was angry"; and in a prayer, which was rather a remonstrance against Jehovah's mercy, he said: "O Jehovah, was not this my saying, when I was yet in my country? Therefore I hastened to flee to Tarshish; for I knew that thou art a gracious God, and full of compassion, slow to anger, and plenteous in mercy, and repentest thee of the evil" (4.1–2). This shows that he fled to Tarshish because he did not believe that God would destroy the city. He believed that even after its doom was pronounced, God's grace, compassion, and mercy would lead him to spare the great population, and that his own mission would therefore appear to be a failure. This reasoning shows plainly that if he had been sure that the destruction of the city would follow, he would have gone; and why? Undoubtedly because Jonah, in common with his countrymen, hated the Ninevites, and would have been glad to witness their destruction. That proud city had sent forth its desolating armies into neighboring kingdoms, through mere lust of conquest, and had aroused the intensest hatred of every conquered nation, and no less that of every nation which sympathized with the oppressed. While God, then, was moved by the grace, compassion, and mercy of which Jonah speaks so admirably and desired through the ministration of Jonah to bring the Ninevites to repentance, that he might save them, the preacher whom he chose was full of hatred toward them, and refused to go because he desired their destruction. Jonah but reflected the sentiments of all Israel; and this brings prominently to view another problem for Jehovah to work out, the riddance of his own people of a feeling so unworthy, not to say degrading. We shall see in the sequel that the aim at this riddance played an important part in directing the course of events.

Jonah's flight to Joppa, whence he expected to set sail for Tarshish, covered a distance of not less than one hundred miles. He doubtless traveled rapidly, and his mental agitation must have been extreme; for he had reason to fear at every step some providential interference with his attempt to escape God's command. But when he found passage in a ship, and was far out at sea with every prospect of a favorable voyage, his excitement naturally subsided, and nervous depression followed. He sought his berth, and fell asleep. So profound was his sleep, that when the storm arose even the tossing of the vessel did not awake him. The master of the vessel was astonished to find him asleep under such circumstances, and calling him a "sleeper," he cried: "What meanest thou, O sleeper? Arise, call upon thy God, if so be that he will think upon us, that we perish not." The cry was like a thunderclap to Jonah. He rushed on deck to find that while he slept such a tempest had fallen on the ship as threatened its destruction; that the sailors had cast the freight into the sea to lighten the vessel; that every one had then called mightily upon his god for safety; and that they had just agreed to cast lots that they might know God whose account this evil had come upon them. The true cause flashed across Jonah's mind in an instant; but he had nerve enough to join in the casting of lots. When he drew the black ball from the urn, he was immediately plied with questions faster than he could answer them: "What is thine occupation? Whence comest thou? What is thy country? Of what people art thou?" When they gave him a chance to speak, he confessed the whole truth: "I am a Hebrew, and I fear Jehovah, the God of heaven, who made the sea and the dry land. I flee from the presence of Jehovah." His questioners had perhaps never before heard of this God—a God who made the sea and the dry land—and when they heard that it was He who had been offended, they were it "exceedingly afraid." If the God who made the sea had raised the tempest against them, what could they do? Believing what Jonah confessed, and naturally thinking that his knowledge of this God would enable him to judge what would appease his wrath, they demand of him: "What shall be done unto thee, that the sea may be calm for us?" This demand put Jonah to the test of all the manliness that was in him. Had he been a coward, or a sneak, he would have begged the sailors to let him remain on board till the ship went to pieces. But he was too manly to permit others to perish on his account, and too honest, now that God had overtaken him, to try to escape the fate which he deserved. To the surprise of all, he answered:

"Take me up and cast me forth into the sea; so shall the sea be calm unto you: for I know that for my sake this great tempest is upon you." Generosity begets generosity. As he was unwilling for them to suffer on his account, they generously resolved not to save themselves at the expense of his life. They turn again to their abandoned oars, and "rowed hard to get back to land." Their efforts are in vain. The sea grows more and more tempestuous against them, and they see clearly that the God who made the sea is determined to have his own way, as declared by Jonah. Trained to stand by a comrade to the last, and to perish if need be in the effort to save him, they tremble at the thought of casting even a strange passenger into the sea to save themselves; and fearing lest, even with the clear demonstration before them, they might offend the God whom they were seeking to appease, before they laid hands on Jonah they offered this prayer: "We beseech thee, O Jehovah, we beseech thee, let us not perish for this man's life, and lay not upon us innocent blood, for thou, O Jehovah, hast done as it pleased thee." Thus, for the first time in their lines they prayed to Jehovah, the only true and living God. Then, with the steady step which only trained sailors could command on a vessel tossed as that one was, they took Jonah, several men seizing him from either side, walked to the rail and cast him into the boiling sea. The vessel sped on its way and they saw him no more. The wild tempest sank to a moderate breeze, the tossing waters stretched themselves out in a gentle swell. "The sea ceased from her raging." The effect upon the seamen was irresistible: "Then the men feared Jehovah exceedingly; and they offered a sacrifice unto Jehovah, and made vows." It is not necessary to suppose that they waited till they went ashore before they offered this sacrifice. They could erect an altar on the deck of the ship and offer such victims as they had on board; and, if neither their altar nor the victim was such as the Mosaic law required, of which they knew nothing, they could hope for acceptance. The vows they made were doubtless vows to serve Jehovah.

Thus far the flight of Jonah has resulted in some good—in the conversion of these seamen to the worship of Jehovah. And did the good work stop with them? Did they not tell the story in every seaport visited by their ship in its long voyage? Did not every one of them continue to tell the strange and glad story as long as he lived? This ship's company, we may safely assert, were made missionaries to the heathen, preaching the true God in all the seaports of the Mediterranean, and thus a light was kindled in the dark places of the western world.

But leaving this part of the story, which grows on our imagination as we dwell upon it, we return to Jonah. When he was cast headforemost into the raging sea, he undoubtedly believed that it was a plunge into hell, for he was caught in the midst of his sin, and now he faces instant death. But he finds himself sliding down the cold throat of a great fish, of whose widespread jaws he barely caught a glimpse ere he passed within them. He is in the bowels of the fish, with every limb cramped as in a vice. He can not breathe, though he struggles for breath desperately. He suffers the pangs of the dying in every nerve and muscle. He realizes the plunge of the great animal into the deep waters; he hears the scraping of seaweeds on its sides; and, as the fish, now full of pain and alarm caused by the struggles of a living man within him, rushes hither and thither in his fury, Jonah is conscious of all his movements. What was his sense of time? He tells us, and in the same breath he reveals the anguish which his soul experienced. He exclaims: "The earth with her bars closed upon me *forever*. Out of the belly of Sheol I cried." He expected every moment to be his last; he was already suffering in body and mind the very torments of the damned; every slow moment as it passed appeared like years, every day like a cycle of eternity.

Suddenly he feels the warm sun in his face. He opens his eyes. He sees the dry land around him, and down below is the sea. The fish is gone, and this seems to be the shore of his native land. How long he lay there before he acquired strength to rise and walk; whether he was found there in helpless weakness by some passerby, or made his way unassisted to some dwelling where he might procure food and drink, we are not informed. We are left equally in the dark as to how long it took him to get back to his home in Gath-hepher, and as to the way in which the news of his adventure was spread abroad. The remarkable reticence which characterizes all of the sacred records, and which distinguishes them from all fictitious writings, is strikingly prominent here. But now that the prophet has been delivered, and is restored to home and family for a time, we may pause and look back with the question, is this his mode of return incredible?

We can not be mistaken in affirming that God, having formed the purpose of bringing the Ninevites to repentance, was not to be defeated. Having selected the man through whose preaching the good work was to be accomplished, he was not to be outwitted by that man. The runaway preacher must be brought back. God could have caused the wind to blow in such a direction as to force back the slip, or he could have seized Jonah by the hair of the head, and brought him back to Gath-hepher; but neither of these methods, nor any other that I can think of, would have been so wise as the one stated in the story. No other would have involved so complete a conversion of the heathen sailors; no other could have taught Jonah so good a lesson; and none, except the second just mentioned, could have brought him back so quick. The fish ran faster than any ship afloat, and even the ocean racers of the present day would have been left by him far in the lurch. Jonah learned, and through his valuable experience millions have learned, that when God enjoins a disagreeable duty, it is far easier to go and do it than to run away from it. It was an act worthy then of Him who sees all things in all places, and who is ever-watchful to provide for all the foreseen generations of men the instruction which they need. The far-reaching effects of the event in the moral training of the world removes it as far as the east is from the west away from the category of idle wonders. And this is not all. We may safely say that if Jonah had gone to Nineveh when the word of Jehovah first came to him, his preaching would have been in vain; for though he would have come as a great prophet, he would not have been "a sign to the Ninevites," in the sense in which our Lord, as we have seen, uses that expression; and lacking this element of power, his mission would have been a failure. God knew this; for he knows all things. He knew that Jonah would run away as he did; he intended from the beginning to bring him back as he did; and all this was necessary to the effective execution of his benevolent purpose to save the Ninevites. From every possible point of view the whole scheme was worthy of God, and I confidently affirm that the story could not have been invented by man. No myth, no legend, in the whole range of human literature, can compare with it in all the elements which make it an incident worthy of divine interposition. If any man doubts this assertion, let him select his example and present it for comparison.

We are not informed how long Jonah remained at home before God spoke to him again; and this is another example of the reticence quite unnatural to fiction, which characterizes this narrative. It may have been a day, a week, or a month; but when the chosen moment came, God spoke to Jonah again. He says nothing about the first command, about the flight to Joppa, about the storm at sea, about the fish. He says, as if for the first time, "Arise, go unto Nineveh, that great city, and preach unto it the preaching that I bid thee." There is no flight or hesitation this time. "Jonah arose and went to Nineveh." Why this change? Has he altered his opinion as to whether or not God will destroy the city? Is the distance to Nineveh any less than it was before? Is the journey any less expensive or laborious? Ah, Jonah has learned the lesson of implicit obedience, the lesson of leaving all consequences with God. He goes to Nineveh. As he goes, I confess for my own part, that if the story of Jonah had closed here without another word, I would be constrained to regard it as one of the most valuable of all the episodes in the Old Testament.

When he began to cry out in the streets of Nineveh, "Yet forty days and Nineveh shall be overthrown," the question necessarily went from lip to lip, Who is this? The answer, that it was the great prophet of Israel, by whose supernatural foresight the victories of Jeroboam, running through a period of forty years, had been won, was enough to arrest solemn attention; but when it was added that on first receiving the command to come and utter this cry, he tried to escape the task by running away, and sailing far out upon the sea, but that Jehovah, who had given the command, overtook him, brought him back in the bowels of a fish, cast him out alive on dry land, and then renewed the command, this added tenfold power to the word of the prophet. The Ninevites believed, proclaimed a fast, put on sack-cloth, turned every man from his evil way, and called mightily on Jehovah. Is this incredible? I have tried to think what effect such a proclamation, by such a man, under such circumstances, would have in our modern society; and I can think of only one class of persons who would probably not repent, and that is the class made up of men who have listened to the gospel for years and years, heard it in all its power, in all its tenderness, and have so hardened their hearts by continued resistance to it, that nothing less than the thunders of the judgment day is likely to bring them to repentance. Men untrained to such resistance, as were the Ninevites, men who had never in their lives before been confronted with the outspoken wrath of the Almighty, could only tremble and repent and pray. The repentance of the Ninevites was natural. Most unnatural is the impenitence of the gospel-hardened sinners of our own day.

But the effect of Jonah's preaching could not, in the nature of things, be confined to the people of Nineveh. Throughout the Assyrian empire, and wherever on earth the name of Nineveh was known, the influence of her example must have been felt; and the revelations of eternity alone will enable us to know how much good was accomplished. It would not be strange if many souls unknown to fame, both in Nineveh and elsewhere, were brought to lasting repentance and finally to eternal life. Jonah was a great missionary to the heathen, and we may be sure that his work was not in vain.

How Jonah ascertained that God "repented of the evil that he said he would do unto the Ninevites," we are not informed; and this is another instance of the reticence common to this and other books of the Bible. But when he did ascertain it he was angry; and he gave vent to his anger by exclaiming: "O Jehovah, was not this my saying when I was yet in my own country? Therefore I hasted to flee unto Tarshish; for I knew that thou art a gracious God, and full of compassion, slow to anger, and plenteous in mercy, and repentest thee of the evil. Therefore now, O Jehovah, take, I beseech thee, my life from me; for it is better for me to die than to live." God answered him, "Doest thou well to be angry?" sad here the interview ended.

One would have supposed that Jonah would return to his home, having accomplished the mission on which he was sent; but instead of doing this, he "went out of the city, and sat on the east side of the city, and there made him a booth, and sat under it in the shadow, till he might see what would become of the city." Why had he any question as to what would become of the city, when God had repented of the evil which he said he would do it? I can think of no answer, unless it be that he had no confidence in the repentance of the Ninevites. They had been so desperately wicked that their sudden repentance appeared more like a spasm of fright than a genuine turning away from sin; and he did not believe it would last. If it did not, if they turned back to their old ways, he knew very well that God would certainly bring upon them the doom which had been pronounced. What was to become of the city, then, depended upon the genuineness and the permanency of the reformation which had been effected; and Jonah, still wishing to see his prediction fulfilled, determines to await the result. He must wait till at least forty days expire, and possibly longer; but the presumption is that he intended to remain only through the forty days.

Instead of taking up his temporary abode within the city walls, he chose a point of observation in the plain to the east, and probably it was the summit of some elevation from which he could have an extended view. The booth which he built was not to keep off the wind or the rain; but to shelter him from the heat, which is very intense in that region during the hot season. It was not made of leaves, which would wilt and curl in a single day under such heat; but of sticks and small boards which he could pick up in the vicinity. It afforded a very imperfect shelter from the direct rays of the sun, and none from the reflected heat which rose from the surrounding sand. He suffered much, but God had pity on him, and "prepared a gourd, and made it to come up over Jonah, that it might be a shadow over his head, to deliver him from his evil case." That gourd sprang up in a single night, so that it might appear, as it was, a special and miraculous gift from God. Jonah was "exceedingly glad because of the gourd." Doubtless it covered the whole of the shanty which had so imperfectly sheltered him, shutting out the side heat as well as the direct rays of the sun, and giving him the full benefit of any breeze that might blow. But the relief lasted only one day. The next morning God having prepared a worm that smote the gourd, when the sun became hot its leaves wilted, turned yellow, curled up, and dropped off. When the heat of the day had come Jonah suffered more than ever. "The sun beat upon the head of Jonah, that he fainted, and requested for himself that he might die." He was now angry again; and God said to him, "Doest thou well to be angry for the gourd?" He said "I do well to be angry, even unto death." I suppose that he meant, he was so angry that it would kill him if he did not get relief. He does not claim to be angry with God, or with the Ninevites, or with any person or thing in particular. It was one of those fits of anger to which many persons are subject when suffering, and which makes them growl and snarl like a wild beast in pain.

The opportunity had now come; God had brought about the opportunity to teach Jonah the last lesson for which this series of events was projected. Had Nineveh been destroyed he would have gone home happy. His present misery was brought on in consequence of his desire to see it destroyed even yet. He was displeased with the mercy which God had manifested toward it, and refused to believe that this mercy would continue. So God says to him: "Thou hast had pity on the gourd, for which thou hast not labored, neither madest it to grow; which came up in a night, and perished in a night: and should not I have pity on Nineveh, that great city, wherein are more than six score thousand persons that can not discern between their right hand and their left hand; and also much cattle?"

What a rebuke for the unfeeling hostility of the prophet toward a vast population; and what forgetfulness it displayed on his part of the multitude of innocent babes who would have been swallowed up in the destruction which he desired to witness! The rebuke was instantaneous; but what shall we say of the train of thought which it awoke in Jonah's mind never to cease while he lived? And when the knowledge of this last scene came to spread abroad in Israel, who can tell the good impression made on thoughtful minds, as day after day and year after year the thrilling story was told, and God's chosen people were made to realize that he was not their God only, but the God of the whole earth?

If now we review the whole story in the light of our reflections on it, we see that it represents God as desiring the repentance of the Ninevites, and of all in the proud empire of Assyria who could be influenced by their example. He selects as the preacher through whose word this great reformation may be effected, the most renowned prophet of the age. Knowing in advance that this prophet, great as he was, would be moved by his knowledge of God's goodness, and his own hatred of Nineveh, to run away from the task assigned him, God permits him to flee far out upon a stormy sea, that he might make him the means there of turning a company of heathen sailors to the true faith, and send them preaching round the shores of the western world, and that he might at the same time bring the prophet back better than ever prepared to do effective work in Nineveh. As a result of this preparation, the whole population of the great city is brought to repentance, and they appeal so earnestly to Jehovah for mercy that he spares them after having doomed them to destruction. We need no historian's pen to assure us that as far as Nineveh was known, the news of this thrilling experience traveled with the speed of the wind; and that an impression in favor of fearing and honoring Jehovah must have been made on every mind. What could have been more worthy of God than all this? Then, that he might send the prophet back to his countrymen with a new and kindlier sense of the brotherhood of man springing out of this universal Fatherhood of God, the weary waiting on the sand hill follows, and the whole story terminates with the tender lesson drawn from the magic shade which refreshed the suffering prophet. Is the story incredible? I think my readers are ready to answer, Not if any other miracles are credible.

But there is another side to the question of incredibility. If the story of Jonah is not history, it is, of course, a piece of fiction, and fiction which originated in the brain of an Israelite. Now I think it may be made to appear that the latter alternative is incredible. It is incredible, in the first place, that any Israelite, capable of conceiving and of writing such a story, would be so irreverent toward one of the great prophets of his nation as to make him act the part ascribed to Jonah. And even if an intellectual Israelite had been so recreant to the ordinary traditions of his countrymen as to write such a story, it is still more incredible that the leaders of the chosen people at any period of their history would have allowed such a document a place among their sacred books. There is nothing of the kind to be found elsewhere in the Bible, and such aspersions upon the names of prophets or patriarchs is not to be found in the apocryphal literature of the Jews. On the contrary, the Jewish writings which are known to be fictitious are often characterized by extravagant eulogies of Biblical characters.

This alternative is incredible, in the second place, because no Israelite, inventing, a story of God's dealings with a great Gentile city like Nineveh, would have represented him as being so regardful of the welfare of its people, so quick to forgive their sins, and so tenderly mindful of the innocent within its walls. Especially would no Israelite write a story whose culminating point was a stern rebuke of his nation for animosity toward an oppressive heathen power. From this point of view, as well as from the other, such a book, if written as a fiction, would have so outraged the feeling of zealous priests and scribes that it would never have obtained a place in the sacred canon. How can we imagine that a people who attempted to slay Jesus because he showed them that a Gentile woman and a Gentile warrior, in the days of Elijah and Elisha, honored these two prophets as no man or woman in Israel did or would, have permitted a book so full of rebuke for their hatred of the heathen to be made a part of their own Bible? The thought is preposterous. Yet, this is the alternative to which those are driven who affirm that the story as told in the Scriptures is incredible. Like unbelievers in general, they take the harder side.

This incredibility is intensified when we consider the date assigned to the Book of Jonah by those who hold it to be fictitious. According to Dr. Driver, as we have seen, it was written in the fifth century BC, after the return from the Babylonian captivity. Nineveh, at that time, together with the Assyrian Empire of which it was the head, had long since perished; yet, this book, though dealing with its sins and its doom, gives not a hint of its final fate. This reticence, if the assumed date is the real one, could have been assumed by its author only for the purpose of making it appear that the book was written before Nineveh's fall; and it was, therefore, a piece of deception. As Nineveh had not only perished at this date, but had, between the time of Jonah and the time of its downfall, carried into captivity the ten tribes of Israel, and visited upon them unspeakable cruelties, a Jew of a later age would be the last man on earth to invent a story showing tender regard for it on the part of Israel's God. Furthermore, at the supposed date of composition, the whole of the twelve tribes, with the single exception of the remnant who had returned to Jerusalem, were being ground under the heel of heathen oppression, and were learning to hate the ways of the oppressors more and more with every passing day. In no former period in Israel's history was it so improbable that such a book could be written by an Israelite, or that, if written, it would be received with any feeling but abhorrence by his countrymen. In other words, the farther down the stream of time you bring the date of the book, the more incredible it is that any Jewish writer would have invented its story, and the more incredible that it could have obtained the place which we know it did obtain in the sacred writings of the Jews. To bring the matter nearer home, let us suppose that some ingenious writer should now publish a volume containing aspersions upon the character of one of the leading generals or statesmen of our revolutionary war, and rebuking severely as unjust and cruel the feeling of the American patriots toward their British foes; and suppose that, by common consent of this generation of Americans, these sentiments should come to he incorporated in the standard histories of the United States. This would be a state of things not one whit more incredible, not to say impossible, than the theory that the Book of Jonah is a fictitious narrative written by an uninspired author in an age of Jewish subjection to a heathen power.

Finally, when we add to the incredibility of the theory that this book is a fiction, the solemn assertion by Jesus that its leading incidents are real transactions, we can safely conclude this protracted discussion with the affirmation, that none of the supernatural events recorded in the Old Testament are supported by stronger evidence of authenticity than those recorded in the Book of Jonah.

4. The Three Days and Three Nights

The words of Jesus, "As Jonah was three days and three nights in the bowels of the sea monster, so shall the Son of man be three days and three nights in the heart of the earth," are very puzzling to many modern readers because of their apparent inconsistency with the accounts given elsewhere of the time between his death and his resurrection. That he was buried on Friday evening, and that he arose on Sunday morning, is so clearly set forth in the Gospel narratives, and so generally accepted as true, that it must be acknowledged as a settled fact. But this is totally irreconcilable with the statement that he was three days and three nights in the heart of the earth, if the latter is to be understood in the sense now attached to the words. Some scholars have thought the contradiction to be real, and have for this reason thought that the verse containing the words ascribed to Jesus are an interpolation in Matthew's Gospel; while others have been driven to novel theories as to the time Jesus spent in the tomb. Many attempts have been made to show that there is no real contradiction; but the most of these have proved unsatisfactory. It is the purpose of this essay to make another such attempt, and I trust that the reader will find it supported by competent and sufficient evidence.

The contradiction between the statement made and the facts recorded is so palpable from the point of view of our English usage, that if the two are harmonious the harmony must be found in some peculiar usage of Hebrew writers and speakers—a usage by which the expression three days and three nights is the equivalent of a small part of one day, all of the next, and a part of the third. Such usage would appear very strange to us, but if it really existed among the Hebrews its strangeness can not nullify it. Its existence must not be assumed in order to get rid of a difficulty of interpretation; it must be demonstrated independently of the passage in which the difficulty is found. Can this be done?

It was the invariable custom of Hebrew writers to count a fraction of a year, or a day, at the beginning of a series and at the end of it, as each a year, or a day. This can be demonstrated by many examples and especially by the parallel numbers recorded in the Books of Kings. Abijam began to reign over Judah in the eighteenth year of Jeroboam; he reigned three years, and yet he died in the twentieth year of Jeroboam (1 Kgs 15.1–2, 8–9). Evidently the three years are made up by a part of Jeroboam's eighteenth, all of his nineteenth, and a part of his twentieth. Nadab began to reign over Israel in the second year of Asa, and reigned two years, yet he died in the third year of Asa (15.25, 28). His two years were a part of Asa's second, and a part of his third; and they may have been not more than one whole year. In the same third year of Asa, Bassha began to reign, and reigned twenty-four years, yet he died in the twenty-sixth year of Asa, one year too soon in our mode of counting (15.33; 16.6, 8). Elah began in the twenty-sixth year of Asa, reigned two years and died in the twenty-seventh of Asa (8–10). This method is pursued till the fall of the northerly Kingdom without variation; and the consequence is, that in estimating the duration of the two kingdoms of Israel and Judah by the regnal years of their kings, it is necessary to deduct at least half a year from the given number of every one who reigned more than one year. Even then the result is in some degree uncertain; for we can never know what part of a year is counted in individual instances, as a year. To this extent Hebrew chronology is uncertain, though the uncertainty is confined within narrow limits.

That the same custom prevailed in regard to days is proved by a large number of examples. Joseph put his brothers "into ward three days"; yet he released them "the third day" (Gen 42.17–18).

By our count he would have released them the fourth day. Rehoboam said to the people who had petitioned him to make their burdens lighter, "Depart yet three days, then come again to me"; yet the historian says, "Jeroboam and all the people came to Rehoboam, the third day as the king bade, saying, Come to me again the third day." Here it is clear that a part of the day in which he dismissed them, all of the next day, and the early part of the day in which they came back to him, make up the three days; yet there were probably less than two days according to our mode of counting. Esther sent word to Mordecai, "Go gather together all the Jews that are present in Shushan, and fast for me, and neither eat nor drink three days, night or day; I also and my maidens will fast in like manner; and so will I go in until the king"; yet she went in on the third day (Est 4.16; v 1). Here are three examples taken from the Old Testament. There are others in the new. Cornelius said to Peter, "Four days ago, until this hour, I was keeping the ninth hour of prayer in my house"; yet if we count from the time of his prayer as stated in the beginning of the story, we find that it was exactly three days according to our mode of counting. He was praying in the afternoon at the ninth hour when the angel appeared to him (Acts 10.3); he immediately started the soldier and the two servants for Peter (7–8); they reached the house where Peter was lodging the next day at noon (9) not quite one day after the vision; Peter has them to stay all night, and the next day they all start for Caesarea (23); and on the next day at the ninth hour they meet Cornelius (24, 30). In order to make the four days, he counted less than three hours of the first day, the whole of the second and third, and nine hours of the fourth. In this instance we have to deduct exactly twenty-four hours from the number of days given in order to have the exact number. Again, the chief priests and the Pharisees, after the burial of Jesus, say to Pilate, "We remember that that deceiver said while he was yet with us, After three days I will rise again. Command, therefore, that the sepulcher be made sure until the third day" (Matt. 27.63–64). Why say "till the third day," if he was to rise *after three days?* We would have said, till the fourth day; for if he was to rise after three days it would not be earlier than the fourth day, though it might be later. Evidently they understood the time included in the expression after three days as terminating on the third day. And as Jesus had been buried near the close of a day, and they expected him to rise, if at all, on the third day, they must have counted the small fraction of a day that remained after his burial as one of the three days. Their expression, "till the third day," also shows that they expected him to rise before the third day would end, and that they therefore count a part of that day as a day.

Finally, Jesus himself had the same usage in his own references to the time between his death and his resurrection; for he at one time says that he would rise on the third day, and at others, that he would rise after three days. See Mark 8.31; 9.31; 10.34, for the latter; and Matthew 16.21; 17.23; 20.19; Luke 9.22; 18.33; 24.7, 46, for the former.

Now of the passages cited, it is only those in Mark which contain the words, "after three days"; while the parallels in Matthew and Luke have the words, "the third day." If we understand that Jesus in every instance used the words given in Matthew and Luke, then we must understand that Mark construes his expression "on the third day," as the equivalent of "after three days." And on the other hand if the expression which Mark has is the literal quotation from Jesus, then Matthew and Luke give "on the third day" as the equivalent of that. The Pharisees, as we have seen, understand him as saying, or at least as meaning, that he would rise "after three days"; for such is their expression in addressing Pilate (Matt 27.63).

We are now prepared to consider the particular words of Jesus which are under discussion—"The Son of man shall be three days and three nights in the heart of the earth." We have seen that "after three days," and "on the third day," were equivalents with him and with his contemporaries; but after three days is actually after three days and three nights. To make this very simple, if you begin to count on Monday morning, after one day would bring you to Tuesday morning; after two days brings you to Wednesday morning; and after three days brings you to Thursday morning; but in passing over three days you have also passed over three nights, *viz.*, Monday night, Tuesday night, and Wednesday night. If, then, Jesus could at one time say in strict compliance with Jewish usage, that he would rise after three days, he could with precisely the same meaning say that he would be in the grave three days and three nights. Neither assertion would be true according to modern usage, but both would be strictly true according to the usage of the Hebrews.

This conclusion is confirmed by another consideration. It is this—that when Jewish writers wished to be exact in the use of the cardinal numbers for years, months, *etc.* they used the qualifying term full, or whole, before the substantive. Thus a law in Leviticus provided that if a house in a walled city were sold, the owner might redeem it "within a whole year after it is sold; for a full year shall he have the right of redemption" (25.29). It was after "two full years" that Absalom took revenge on Amnon, and when he returned from banishment on account of slaying Amnon, he dwelt "two full years" in Jerusalem before he saw the king's face. Zedekiah, the false prophet, said that the vessels of the house of the Lord, which had been carried to Babylon, would be brought back within "two full years" (Jer 28.3). Stephen says that Moses was "full forty years old" when he slew the Egyptian and fled. Luke says that Barnabas and Saul remained with the church at Antioch "a whole year," and that Paul dwelt in his own hired house in Rome "two whole years." In view of this usage we can see that if Jesus had meant that he would be in the heart of the earth three days and three nights as we understand the words, he would have said three full days and nights; or if he had meant what we mean by "after three days," he would have said, After three *full* days, or three *whole* days.

If it shall still appear to any one that such a usage is so far from accuracy of expression as to be somewhat incredible, let him consider some usages of our own, which though not the same, are analogous. Suppose that a freshly landed Chinaman were to employ an American laborer for a month, agreeing to pay him twenty dollars. At the end of the month the man claims his wages though he has labored only twenty-six days. The Chinaman would think himself cheated out of four days labor until he was informed that according to American usage a month's labor is not counted at thirty days, but at only twenty-six. Or suppose that he sends his son to an American school which begins the first day of March and is to continue five months. The Chinaman counts the time and expects his son to receive instruction to the end of July, which would be twenty-one weeks and six days. But at the end of twenty weeks the tuition fee is demanded, and he thinks that he has been cheated out of two weeks, until he learns that in American school parlance a month, which he counted as sometimes thirty days, and sometimes as thirty-one, is only four weeks. But worse still, he finds upon careful count that there were two days in every week of the twenty in which his son was not taught; and thus the twenty-one weeks and six days for which he thought he was contracting, has been reduced to just one hundred days or fourteen weeks and two days. He thinks that these Americans have a very strange way of counting time, and he is right in so thinking; yet we go on counting this way without stopping to think how strange it is. So it was with the Jews in their method, and in reality their method did not involve so many and so great inaccuracies as our own. This consideration should silence all cavilling about the method of the Jews, and about the apparently inconsistent statements with reference to the time that our Lord spent in Joseph's tomb.

Also from DeWard Publishing

Heritage of Faith Library

The Man of Galilee
Atticus G. Haygood

Dr. Haygood's apologetic for the deity of Christ using Jesus Himself as presented by the gospel records as its chief evidence. This is a reprint of the 1963 edition. The Man of Galilee was originally published in 1889. 108 pages. $8.99.

Our Brother in Black
Atticus G. Haygood

Originally published in 1881, Our Brother in Black: His Freedom and His Future is Atticus G. Haygood's concise and insightful study of race relations in the post-bellum American South. At the core of Haygood's writing is an unflinching belief that God's hand was in the events expanding African slavery to American shores, the cataclysmic Civil War, and the ill-fated, short-circuited efforts to usher former slaves across the threshold to full citizenship. Central, too, is Haygood's resolution that all men of faith, regardless of skin color, can share common rights and responsibilities within a single free society, working for its progress and defending its liberties.

A Treatise on the Eldesrhip
J.W. McGarvey

McGarvey's brief but thorough study on the eldership, focusing on the work that the shepherds of God's flock need to be doing. While he also discusses theological matters, this is an eminently practical work.

Coming in 2009

A Guide to Bible Study
J.W. McGarvey

Original Commentary on Acts
J.W. McGarvey

DeWard Original Publications

Beneath the Cross: Essays and Reflections on the Lord's Supper
Jady S. Copeland and Nathan Ward (editors)

The Lord's Supper is rich with meaning supplied by Old Testament foreshadowing and New Testament teaching. Explore the depths of symbolism and meaning found in the last hours of the Lord's life in *Beneath the Cross.* Filled with short essays by preachers, scholars, and other Christians, this book is an excellent tool for preparing meaningful Lord's Supper thoughts—or simply for personal study and meditation. 329 pages. $14.99 (PB); $23.99 (HB).

The Growth of the Seed: Notes on the Book of Genesis
Nathan Ward
A study of the book of Genesis that emphasizes two primary themes: the development of the Messianic line and the growing enmity between the righteous and the wicked. In addition, it provides detailed comments on the text and short essays on several subjects that are suggested in, yet peripheral to, Genesis. 537 pages. $19.99.

The Big Picture of the Bible
Kenneth W. Craig
In this short book, the author summarizes the central theme of the Bible in a simple, yet comprehensive approach. Evangelists across the world have used this presentation to convert countless souls to the discipleship of Jesus Christ. Bulk discounts will be available, as will special pricing for congregational orders. 48 pages, color. $4.99.

Boot Camp: Equipping Men with Integrity for Spiritual Warfare
Jason Hardin

According to Steve Arterburn, best-selling author of *Every Man's Battle,* "This is a great book to help us men live opposite of this world's model of man." *Boot Camp* is the first volume in the IMAGE series of books for men. It serves as a Basic Training manual in the spiritual war for honor, integrity and a God-glorifying life. 237 pages, $13.99 (PB); $24.99 (HB).

For a full listing of our titles, visit our website: www.dewardpublishing.com

www.ingramcontent.com/pod-product-compliance
Lightning Source LLC
LaVergne TN
LVHW050942080826
845145LV00004B/1373

* 9 7 8 0 9 8 1 9 7 0 3 2 5 *